Monotonous Children

Carden Michael

Contents

ACKNOWLEDGMENTS

Being trapped in the shadow of death, I give thanks to the Master for rescuing me from Death Valley. He woke me from my slumbering mentality and equipped me with the spoken word, blessing me with the gift of writing poetry, essays, and short stories.

Never did I think I could formulate words and make them into sentences and paragraphs. These inspirations I felt nourished my soul; great are they who publish them.

How could I be ungrateful to him from whence all blessings flow? When I was blind, he sharpened my vision to see things farther than a telescope.

I also give thanks to Nigel Daring, Lloyd Joe, Allan Palmer, and Jimar Harry for their suggestions, and to the editor, Dr. Thomas Dean, for his editorial assistance. You all are awesome.

INTRODUCTION

I personify as a Lion. Yet I am gentle as a butterfly, harmless as a pony, and kind as a dove. Be my guest; you won't regret it.

From the minds of the impish come lies, minimization, humiliation, and victimization. Since I have discovered the gift of writing, detractors have questioned the authenticity of my work. Repudiations could have deterred me from accomplishing my mission, as well as the barriers that plotters set in my way.

Dear friends, can you imagine? A bold, wicked audacious adversary had the audacity to tell me that in order for me to master the art of writing, I had to study literature. Little did he know that within me lies creativity,
Sweet inspiration,
Rhythmical groovy beats,
And thunderous vibration!

You see, I reject the notion that I have to sit in a classroom to learn the so-called science of writing. Why should I have to study another's creation when the Master gave me the natural ability to formulate words into sentences and paragraphs intelligently?

Critics cannot stop me from doing what I came here to do because mystical powers protect me from the minds that conceive disgusting envy and jealousy. They waste their time fighting against me because whenever they do so, they revitalize my spirit, causing me to roar like a lion by becoming more courageous, motivated, and creative.

To date, Monotonous Children *is the fifth book I have written. The others are* Boundless Vision, Bold Truth, A Narrative of the Dry Bones, *and* The Great White Hoax.

Monotonous Children *is a collection of poetry, essays, and short stories. The messages range from philosophical thoughts, spirituality, and social and political topics to quixotic sentimentality. Apart from my books, I have also produced twenty-five tracks of dub poetry on a CD entitled* Wise Men.

In regard to the title Monotonous Children, *I use it to pinpoint the droning of the arts, particularly in music. I think that most of the upcoming artists are not carrying their weight anymore. It's not as before when artists from different musical genres had their own original styles, sweet vocal harmonies, and musical opuses.*

Some of the musical icons of this era were Millie Jackson, Mahalia Jackson, Smokey Robinson, Bob Marley, and Duke Ellington. You can feel the soulfulness in their blues, jazz, reggae, gospel, and soul. I challenge those who aspire to be writers, singers, and painters to dig deep within their soul and bring out the best that they possess.

I hope that you, the reader, find something that motivates, inspires, and stimulates your mind in one way or another. This book is dedicated to friends, enemies, and foes. Peace and blessings to one and all.

Finding Harmony among Hostility

LIBERATION

As I walk the open plains briskly with a hot, enraged temper, looking for sweet emancipated liberty, a voice told me, "Brother man, let not your furious mind delude you into dangerous territory! Please be cautious as you pursue sweet emancipation. The powers that hold the masses in a chokehold won't relinquish their powers easily. They are as merciless as eagle claws and bite viciously with snapping lion's jaws.

"Brother man, go easy. Don't be in a rush to attain liberty. Let wisdom guide you into perilous territory. Plan your attack strategically to break those goddamn walls of oppression!

"Yea, let your words of wisdom awaken the poor and downtrodden out of their consternation, fear, and anxiety. Tell them not to be afraid of those who possess weapons of mass destruction. When all is said and done, the unscrupulous, improper tyrants they refer to as dignitaries fall like vagabonds and indigents, withering as the green grass that fades away."

Looking at the human psyche introspectively, men have become powerless when they give their power to a brutish few who hold them in captivity, such as the unsympathetic Mussolini, Hitler, Stalin, Botha, Kim Jong-un, Saddam, Bush, Dick, and Wolf.

That wise, cognizant voice tells me, "You hostile, enraged one, take it easy. Liberation does not necessarily come from the outburst of smoking guns or from the explosions of crashing bombs, but rather by raising the consciousness of the human psyche to mitigate poverty, ignorance, sickness, and disease."

That voice I heard tells me, "Liberation does not necessarily come from popping guns or destructive bombs but by finding a common denominator that is embedded in love.

"When mind, body, soul, and spirit are free, bondage, oppression, repression, and shackles will fly away.

"When oppressors and mean-spirited tyrants are put asunder, captive men will run wild and free without being told by dictators to walk on a tightrope!

"When Dracula, imps, and vampires flee from the government house, we will have an egalitarian democracy where strife and conflict once reigned supreme."

Oh, thou old impish, dreadful Dracula, it is a liberating feeling when law-abiding citizens are free in a transparent democracy!

While I stood in the open plains, the sweet liberating voice echoed the sentiment. "Freedom, where are you? The poor and suffering who bear the brute force of the oppressor's hand are yearning to be free. They are longing to feel the presence of your warm solace to soothe their haunted, destitute souls!"

Come, don't delay in rescuing the poor and downtrodden from this hellish dungeon! We need to be free. Too long have we been living in captivity.

This captive soul of mine is making an appeal to liberators. This captive soul of mine is loaded with burdens, tears, and sorrows! Oh, my soul wonders if there is any hope for tomorrow. Yea, I crave for a bright and prosperous future where all hungry mouths shall be fed, where they don't have to beg for crumbs of bread.

Though I am constrained with grief, my heart remains playful, hoping for a future where I won't see malnourished babes scarred in diverse places, guns and bombs sniping, escalating every minute of the hour!

In my woes, I pray that weary feet would stop roaming like restless nomads, roaming for bread in perilous places. Hearts would stop aching from loved ones dying cruelly by snipers' bullets!

Yea, my soul takes an in-depth look at what is going on in Sudan, Ethiopia, Somalia, Angola, and other regions of the earth where war and instability are devastating communities.

All across the globe, I see refugee camps while they who perpetuate crimes flow to the United Nations like vultures, echoing big, lofty rhetoric! I said to the flesh eater vultures, get out of the way and let justice reign! Let justice reign so that the sufferers won't feel picks from your ferocious beaks!

With all the genocide that is taking place, the vultures won't find a solution for the pollution. I asked, "Where do we go from here, to paradise or to that hellish place of doom?!"

That same familiar voice continued to ring in my ears, telling me, "Liberation does not always come from sputtering guns or by flaring bombs, but by elevating the human psyche to a spiritual and scientific dimension, to be at oneness with God and nature."

JUSTICE MERCHANT

When the Justice Merchant saw reprisal in diverse
places, he armed himself with words of righteousness.
He fires—Pow! Pow! Pow! Pow!
Rupturing the skunk heart, that unscrupulous no-good
oppressor!

This advocate for freedom
Is equipped with probity, ethics, and morality;
He beckons the sentiments of equity, eliminating
Inequality.

He sounds his trumpet and topples the status quo of
mosquitoes.
He lifts his voice,
Liberating the voiceless from culprits.

This fearless warrior speaks to the masses,
Dismantling the incursion of injustice,
Bigotry, and tyranny.

Sends shockwaves into the house of parliament,
Terrifies the predatory wolves that kill vulnerable
prey.

Justice Merchant, that fearless warrior,
Wins the victory triumphantly.

www.whitespirit.ne

THE VOICE OF THE NOBLES

The voice of the nobles said to me,
I put word, sound, and power in thee!
Go and speak truth to the nations;
Accomplish the mission!

Your purpose is not to seek glorification,
Self-aggrandizement,
And accolades.

When your work is done,
You will be paid by the son.

Go and tell the nations to flee from
Satan!
Go and tell the nation, "Ah goin' to
Annihilate Satan."

THE VICTORY WAS WON

*After the allegations and accusations, the victory was
won.
Here I stand, free as a bird in a tree.
No bars could have held me.
Chains fled from me.
Rascals could not detour my destiny.
Truth evaluates my innocence.
Freedom was mine,
One step away from Hades;
That place is not for me.
They tried; I was not shy.
Abominable lies I did not tell.
Courage persuaded me;
Validity gave me victory.
The judge had no grudge. He was fair.
I had no fear, doubts, or buts about my faith.
I took my stance; upon solid ground I stand.
I kept my cool; I did not act a fool.*

*Penitentiary: no, no, no!
Solitary confinement is not for me!
Freedom surrounds me; I rejoice triumphantly.
Solitude I toppled,
Suddenly despaired, disappeared.
Happily I overpowered my foes,
Defeated their unlawful suit and injunction.
I pierced the hearts and minds of enemies.
A step away from Hades,
Here I stand, free as a birdie in the tree.*

Whistling sweet melody, Tweet! Tweet, Tweet! Tweet!

8

THE PERCEIVED DOTE

I, the perceived dote, was categorically
Defined as a dolt
By nutty-heads.
Relentlessly they vented
Their venomous tongue at me,
Trying to poison a godly creature like me!

In a silent tone,
I, the perceived dote, told
The dippy-heads,
You silly creatures are doomed to hell's
Home!

Yea, they continue to ridicule me.
Repeatedly
They nag and bash me.
"If you do not have a master's degree,
You are scum, buddy."
"If you didn't go to college,
You have no knowledge."
"If you have no academics,
You are a cacodemon."

As they unleashed their fury,
I was unmoved by their ferocity,
Realizing these jackasses were hyped on intolerance,
foolishness, and ignorance!

EDUCATION

Education is concepts, metaphors, and wise sayings. It is that which comes from the depth of the souls of wise men!

These concepts are derived from the Maker of Life. They did not proceed from the confines of structured walls. Rather, they transpired from the heads of those who were inspired to tell the good news. But then it was tucked into books and taught in the classrooms of learning institutions where folks regurgitated and imitated wise men's thoughts!

Education is a way of life. When you feel it, you have to proclaim it to the nations so it can motivate those who lack inspiration, transforming a torpid nation into sophisticated humans. Blessed are they who were chosen to transport these vibrations! Happy are those that take advantage of such a grandiose privilege.

However, I appeal to that showoff gaudy faller—the next time you see me, do not look down on me because I do not have a PhD.

You gaudy puffed-up faller, the next time you see me, do not ask me, "Where is your degree?"

The next time you see me, do not discard me like a bag of garbage.

Education is what you feel. Education is a way of life. When you feel it, go on—teach!

INTELLIGENCE

What is intelligence?

Intelligence is the acumen that God has put into man to think and to be innovative. Intelligence forms and shapes thoughts to bring about the formation of municipalities and big governments, schools and universities, civics, science, and technology.

Intelligence is the inner power that human beings possess to create their autonomy for a higher development. Some people use theirs; others don't. It gives man the capability to think and the ability to be creative. Without it, man is doomed and will not enjoy the pleasures and comforts of life. Intelligent minds think and create. Use yours to the best of your ability.

I conclude that intelligence has nothing to do with memorization because you cloud regurgitated bullshit and turn out being an absolute fool!

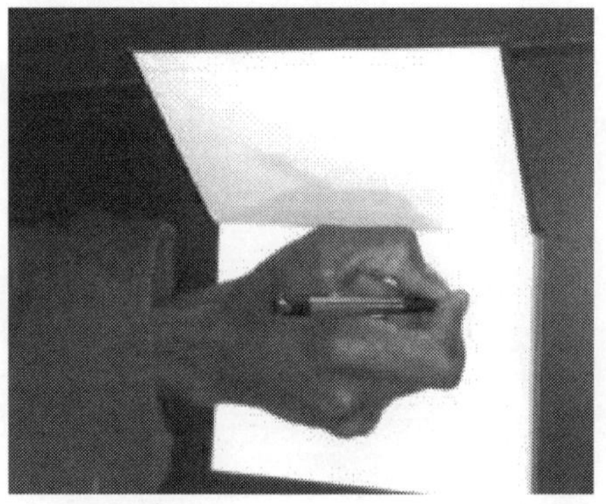

SUCCESS

Success is not for dreamers who succumb to the continuous attacks of nightmares, fantasy, and illusion. Neither is it for procrastinators who fall by the wayside, hoping that something miraculous will suddenly fill their anguished cups. Success is for visionaries who conceptualize by putting their shoulders to the wheel, by pursuing and accomplishing the things that seem impossible for sluggards to achieve.

www.einteinlaw.com

The Sobbing Soul Utters Prayers

I CHANT A PRAYER

I chant a prayer for the man who knows not love,
Hoping he will show compassion and mercy to those
who beg to be pardoned.

I chant a prayer for that fellow who sees not his
imperfection,
Hoping he will search his inner core to behold the
muck that corrodes his retched soul, striving for perfection.

I chant a prayer for that man who stores up earthly
possessions at Swiss banks,
Hoping that he will redistribute some of that which he
had robbed to the motherless, widows, and fatherless.

I chant a prayer for heads of government,
Hoping they will stop using deceptive intelligence and
chicanery to hoodwink the ignorant, blind, and
gullible.
I chant a prayer for the money-hungry preacher to
stop robbing the poor in the name of God,
Hoping they will live by Jesus' example!

I chant a prayer for talebearers and gossipers to
cease from spreading rumors and propaganda,
Hoping their tongues will spread the good news to
heal broken hearts and shattered homes.

I chant a prayer for enemies and foes,
Hoping that we will forgive each other, find a
common denominator by building our foundation
upon love!

BLESSED

Blessed is the mouth that sings songs
To the brokenhearted,
That gives hope to the hopeless,
Comforting those who are in distress.

Blessed is the mouth that sings and tells
The wicked to desist from their evil practices,
Rendering justice to the masses.
Blessed is the mouth that sings freedom songs
uncompromisingly.

BE STRONG

When things seem down and out, and trouble
Surrounds you,
Remember, Jah is standing by, and he knows
Your cries.

When friends desert you,
He will stand by your side.

When the wicked trails your footsteps,
He will not let them get a hold of you.

When you are drowning in sorrow,
He will brighten your tomorrow.

When you are down and out,
Remember, Jah is standing by,
And he will answer your prayers.

HEATHEN

Take heed of the warning.

Be aware, for the time is near.
Hurry up and get on board.

Don't be late
'Cause you will miss the train.
Make haste; shift the gears.

Oh, heathens, be ye not hardened
'Cause in the judgment, you won't have
Time to say "pardon."

Heathen!
Heathen!
Get on board
'Cause this train is bound for Zion's shores.

OH JAH!

Oh Jah!
Marvelous art thou!
The day cannot go by without me falling on my knees,
offering
You prayers.

The heathen declare war on thy name.
They say
There is no supernatural being called Jehovah-Jerit!

Yet the big heads exalt themselves,
Giving themselves numerous titles and expecting
Me to serve them.
The presidents, governors, and crime ministers expect
me to praise them.
Rascals and rogues expect me to worship them.
They've got to be mad!
They've got to be mad!

I heard misguided fools denounce the existence of
your
Heavenly Kingdom,
Yet heads of state build themselves earthly kingdoms
And are adored, praised, and glorified.
They rule with an iron fist and justify themselves for
doing so.

Ah! What a day it will be when presumptuous sinners
Drop on their knees and cry out for mercy.

What a day it will be when the "acute astute"
intellectual fools
Run for cover when they see the devastation of their
earthly
Empires crumble!
Ah! What a day it will be
When they shall see the engulfing fire ravaging their
kingdoms!

What a day it will be,
What a day it will be
To see fire ravaging ravenous men's kingdoms.

Oh Jah!
Oh Jah!
Your judgment is inevitable.

THE WISE MAN

The wise man sits in the glory of his heavens.
He speaks to fools in their arrogance.
Fools comprehend not the words of the wise man
Yet rather choose arrogance as their guiding light.

The lips of the wise man speaks to me the words of
wisdom,
Knowledge, and understanding;
Fools have no delight in knowledge.

Knowledge,
Knowledge,
I prefer you more than that which comes from the
Confinement of college.

Knowledge,
Knowledge,
You are my hierarchy and colleague
In this earthly, haughty dungeon!

SOUND OF SILENCE

*To hear the sound of silence is better than the
Hullabaloo that comes from the house of
Parliament.*

*To hear the sound of silence is better than the
Uproar that comes from the dwellings of
Tenements.*

*To hear the sound of silence is like sailing in the
Tranquility of heaven.*

*To hear the sound of silence is to hear the voice
Of God speaking to my core.*

*To hear the sound of silence sounds good to me.
To hear the sound of silence
Rejuvenates my soul.*

The Gift of Love

SHE ASKED

The lonely, solitary woman asked,
Are you originally from Brooklyn?
I answered no!
I am from St. Vincent and the Grenadines,
Located in the eastern Caribbean Sea.

This is an island that has captured the
Imagination of pirates and buccaneers.
I told her,
It is indeed a majestic grandeur;
Come and taste of her magical wonders.
Many voices say,

"It is the natural place to be."
Come and feel the warmth of hospitality
And see the descendants of Chatoyer, East Indians,
Europeans, and Africans in St. Vincent.

Come and see
The magical wonders that God has bestowed upon
her,
The cascading of seas and beautiful
Beaches,
Scenery and luscious vegetation.
Come and see!
This is a serene place you would like to be.

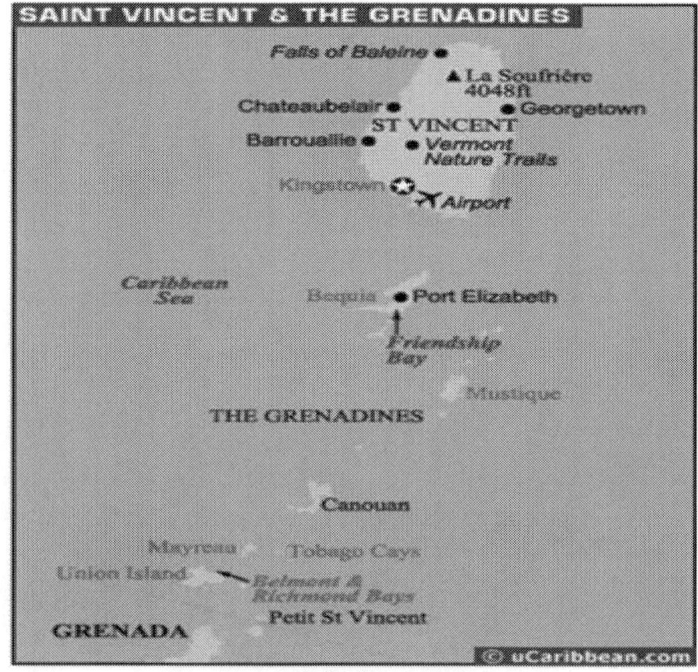

www.infoplease.com

TO A MOTHER

To a mother who is caring.

You are the pillar that supports your family.
You are committed, compassionate, and intelligent,
A fortifier who gives strength and nourishment to her
children,
A caretaker who devotes her time and patience
unselfishly,
A fortress that shelters her children from the raging
storm,
A mother who possesses the strength of a giant,
Deserves to be treated like a royal.

MAMMA

Mamma was a blessing to my soul. She nurtured my growth and taught me the value of life— not to be complacent, lackadaisical, and lazy, but to be ambitious by working hard and accomplishing the good things in life.

In a soft and comforting voice, she told me, "Son, you must never be envious or desirous of other people's wealth. You see that lady who lives next to us in her mansion? She worked very hard for what she has; she alone supported her six boys without a husband.

"Son, sometimes we see people have things, but we don't know how they got them."

I cherish the beauty of Mamma's soul and the wise counsel she imparted to me. They are deep in my memory and intensify the qualities she planted in me.

Yes, I remember the many nights when cavities acted up and had me weeping and groaning, hindering my sleep. She would mix remedies to counteract the pain with me sighing in agony.

Mamma's love was sweet. She was sent from above as a good steward to bring joy and happiness to my soul.

As matriarch and leader of her pride, she gave her lions and lionesses lots of love. She explained to them the basic fundamental principles of hunting in order to prepare them for their survival. Her love was abundant and immeasurable; no doubt, it was refined by heaven.

Although her heart was delicate and sweet, she had a husband who was her opposite, mentally deranged and mean-spirited. He made her life a living hell. Many nights, she wept bitterly as she endured cruelty from that heartless beast who eventually abandoned his family.

Nevertheless, Mamma worked hard and did her best to see that her children were secure and comfortable. She farmed and cultivated vegetables, selling them to traffickers and market vendors. Mamma was a devout Methodist who sang well and participated in the church choir. On numerous occasions, she would participate in singing competitions in the city and won prizes. When she sang, her voice sounded notes like the melodious nightingale that serenaded my soul, especially when she washed our clothes and sung from the sankey "hymnbook."

When it came to cooking, she knew how to stir in the kitchen, bubbling pots making a variety of colorful dishes. Her culinary artistry was tasty, full of flavors, yummy, and delicious. Her flair was as good as any five-star restaurant. Some of her specialties were callaloo soup and paleau. She brewed sour sap juice and lime juice, mauby and lemonade. These were some of the delicacies she used to make.

In our yard, there were always some sorts of animals: goats, pigs, and rabbits. At times, Mamma would improvise, taking scraps and making socks or anything wearable. Life was hard! Nevertheless, she would strategize by making preparations for the rough and critical days ahead. She had the motivation and did not rely on the government even though we were poverty-stricken and victims of colonialism. Yet she put her shoulder to the wheel and headed to the mountain to cultivate her plot of land in order to create a heavenly atmosphere for her children.

Some of my most profound and cherished memories were of Christmas and Easter when there were many moments of leisure and plenty to eat. I would patiently anticipate the arrival of Mom when she went to the city because there were always goodies she would bring back to dazzle my eyes.

As a devout Christian woman, she taught us good morals and the importance of living a spiritual life. Many times she would extend her hands to strangers without hesitation. On Sundays, she would dress us in our Sunday best and send us to Sunday school to learn the golden rule so that we might not turn out to be thugs, rude boys, and bandits.

Mamma was a graceful matriarch. She knew how to dress and carried herself appropriately with respect, dignity, and high self-esteem. In return, neighbors and strangers admired her and called her Mother because of the qualities she possessed.

I love my mother to the max for her contributions to my growth. Mamma's love was a blessing to so many souls.

WOMEN

What would we do without you?
You are the ones who cherish your children with your tender touch.

You run the homes and teach us values and the true essence of love. Yet it saddens my heart when men abuse you and see you as nothing. When the nights come, we seek the fortune you possess, we curve our arms around your tender frame, whispering lies and fairy tales in your ears.

Oh, you lovely, sumptuous women, your honey we cannot do without even though it may be frail, fluffy, or skinny. We should thank you for nourishing our hearts with the tender spot. Nevertheless, I thank the Great Spirit for everything you have. Women, I have heard many sad stories that have made my heart twinge.

Yet you continue to strive despite persecution, battery, and adversity. I adore you princesses, empresses, and queens for the contributions you have made. I pay homage to all nice and decent women. Women! What would life be without you?

SWEET AND ADORABLE QUEEN

Sweet and adorable queen,
How are you?
My knees shudder, tremble, crumble,
And bow to you.
Your poise stimulates my nerves.
How could I have avoided your sustenance and the
Edible nourishment you brought to me?
Still, I crave for more of you and desire your highest
quality goodies.
My thoughts are unstable; they stumble like a
Battered ship
That searches for a place of rest.
I am tossed up and down, looking for a place to rest
My feet on solid
Ground.
I yearn and search for you, my love.
Sweet and adorable queen,
Why won't you come and feel my squeeze?

WHEN YOU ARE LOVED

*When you are loved,
Why blues twisting your countenance into gloom?
When you are loved,
Why sigh running rivers of tears from your eyes?
When there is love,
Why set the notion into a commotion?
When you are loved,
Tell warmongers to drink from the
Fountain of love.*

IF I COME

If I come knocking on your door,
Would you tell me to go to Rome and roam?
Or would you take me in to prickle your thing?
Would you?
Please, honeydew!
Allow me to come in to
Hug you.

ME AND ME CHICK

Me and me chick in the cob,
Doing our thing.
I am very fortunate, having her in my cob.
I can hear her heartbeat;
It sounds sweet, especially when locked away in
private.
She releases stress to no man's land
And causes me to dance like merry men.
Me and me chick in the cob, flapping our wings
And doing our thing.

YOU ARE

32

You are the essence of spices and fragrances.
A rose in the garden, you bloom and sparkle with
elegance.
Your aroma lightens up my heavens.
Thank you, my virtuous virgin. You are a star that
illuminates my nights.

Subtlety in the Psyche

ACTORS OF LIARS

Actors of liars,
Faces of hypocrites, giggles, hee-hee-hee.

Predators, enemies, and foes,

Trumped-up charges of things I never knew.
Hearts of deceivers,
Smiles with golden faces.

Liars and backbiters
Stuck in vain imagination.

Hypocrites, backbiters, and liars still glitter
Their silly faces, hee-hee-hee!!!

CATASTROPHIC MOUTH

Catastrophic mouth,
When would you be wise?
Close your mouth and stop
The snips.

Purify your thoughts
With a renewed heart.

Philosophize
Your thoughts,
And let us talk.

ILLUSION

The price of illusion can be tragic.
I remembered the super fellow
Who flew amongst the stars.
He ended up on Mars,
Flew back to Earth
Affiliated with movie stars.
He rode his horse,
Broke his ass,
Secluded with a broken heart.
Yet I rode my ass and was the commander
Of my colt.
Still, an ass is an ass,
And the darting horse
Ruptured Christopher Reeve's ass!

CREEPS

Creeps love to play hide-and-seek,
Seeking for loved ones to devour,
Searching for happiness to turn into despondency,
Scheming to acquire your wealth for their personal
vanity.
While they are plotting,
I am watching, getting ready for trapping
As they slink, chirp, and crawl along the grass.
I am getting ready for hacking
As they hide and peep.

www.gatpetsonline.com

STRANGE IRONY!

This strange irony might be hard for the unrealistic mind to comprehend!

A few years ago, I gave a diehard communist fifteen of my books to sell. The communist sold my books and concealed the cash like a hardcore capitalist!

Now I am confronted by human deceitfulness. I ask myself, what kind of communist is this guy?

Is he a follower of Karl Marx, Joseph Stalin, or Lenin, or is he an impostor who is fascinated by con-man ideology?

THE FELON

I met a faller who was a felon. I had compassion for the felon,
so I took a chance and gave the felon fifteen watermelons,
hoping that we would split the profits.
The felon sold the melons and ran away.
When he vanished, I said, "My God, that faller is the
most devious of all felons!"

COOK AND CROOK

In my home, I am cook and crook.
I scheme, manipulate, and deceive.
I am so smart; I never get caught by the hook.
Though I scheme, I caution my children to do right.
I tell them, "If you do wrong and get caught,
you will be whopped by the Mighty Hand!"

The Second Chapter of Love

WHEN LOVE IS FOUND

When love is found,
Not even a pearl can take its place.

When love is found,
She deserves to wear gold, sapphire, topaz, and
diamonds.

When love is found,

Womanizers need not drift
Like busybodies in diverse places.

When love is found,
That special someone deserves
A permanent place to sit like a queen on a throne!

SHE GOT FLAVOR

She got flavor,
She got taste.
When I look at her face,
My imagination gets unstable,
Plummeting into diverse places,
Hoping to find a place in her heart
To wiggle my waist.

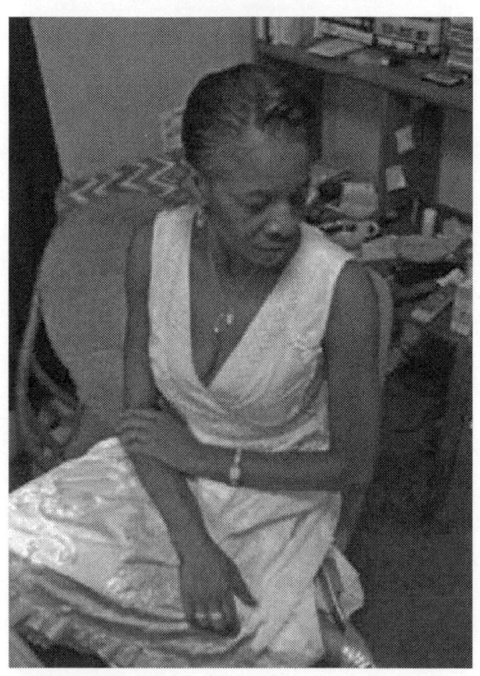

FIRST IMPRESSION

Them say always try to let the first impression
Be the best impression.
But honey, yours is the best!
They do not need judges and critics to judge
And to critique the qualities you possess
'Cause you are the preeminence of what life
Has to exemplify:
Beauty, intelligence, honesty, and virtue!

A LONESOME DOVE

43

A lonesome dove landed upon my windowsill,
I threw my charm and let her in.
I said, "Welcome in, heavenly bird."
From the start,
We began to whistle words of compliments.
Moments later, we were up in our arms, hitting and
Kissing and doing private things.
After she was fed,
I told her not to depart.
"You can enjoy the warmth of my heart."

ROSE IN THE GARDEN

Rose in the garden,
I can smell your aroma from a distance.

Though your fragrance is fit for elegance,
Still I wouldn't sell you for billions.

Even though we are apart,
Still I will be waiting.

Even though babblers' mouth, chat crap,
Faith is the substance of things hoped for.

Even though rumors circulated through the
atmosphere that
I was cheating, still that hasn't set us apart.

Rose in the garden,
Your aroma enthralls my nostrils.

YOUR FREQUENCY

Your frequency so high,
It took me by surprise.

Your frequency so high,
It drew me to you.
When I touch you,
I am consumed by your love.

When I wrap my arms around your waist,
I am hooked on your taste.

When I touch her in the right place,
She tells me to leave it there till the next year!

When passion clamors,
I thank the Great Spirit for my lover.

LOVE YEARNS

Love yearns when she passes by.
Standing next to her, I gaze.

Physique form, luscious and sturdy.
Backside bounces, boom!
Sends off hypnotic waves!
Come, let me hold you, kiss and stroke
You.
Don't be shy or criticize.

Hold me tight and let us cuddle
Throughout the night.

Love yearns in the midst of the night,
Awakens the monstrous beast,
The voracious beater.

SUGARY ADORABLE PRINCESS

A response to a sugary adorable princess:

Of course! I know exactly what you are talking about,
my dear.
I must tell you that I thought about you throughout
the entire weekend.
And I find you to be extraordinarily sweet,
Not like the sugary stuff that rots teeth and gives
diabetes,
But that which gladdens the heart and lights up teeth.
It is said that beauty is in the eye of the beholder.
However, yours shimmers on the inside and outside.
You can steal a king's heart.
Seems like you have stolen mine already.
Take care, Hypnotizer.
It was nice meeting you.

The Lightning Strikes!

MY MOUTH

My mouth is an electrical fire!
See it and leave it.
Love it or hate it.
Touch it, and
It will shock the
Crap out of you!

I RATTLE

Sarcastically I rattle, sending shockwaves through the
Atmosphere.
I prattle not as talebearers,
Nor do I tickle ears like soothsayers,
Promising fake bait to godly saints!

I do not care if you have a spiked nose
Or full nose,

Whether you wear rags or old torn clothes,
Lying in a shack or
Living in a fortress,
Sitting on your fat, crooked ass
With lots of $-cash!

I don't give a damn about your position
Or disposition.

What is meaningful to me is love,
Love!
Love!
Sweet love!
Respect,
Integrity,
Equality and justice;
That's what it takes to refine
Humanity!

THUNDER AND LIGHTNING

I am thunder and lightning.
When I roll, it makes you groan.

When I clap, it makes you gasp.
When I flash, it causes shocks.

When I bolt, it terrifies souls.
When I bang, it makes you run.

When I blast, it chastises thoughts.
When I bash, it makes you dash.

I am thunder and lightning, and
I am frightening.

WARS OF WORDS!

Wars of words can make you and break you,
for I have known a mighty people who were broken and
reduced to scum because of wars of words!
However, when your mind, body, spirit, and soul are
built up with wisdom, knowledge, and understanding,
you can look an intellectual punk in his face and tell him,
"Sucker! I am a man just like you! Get lost!"

WORD, SOUND, AND POWER

Word, sound, and power
Infuriate the wicked heart,
Yet they nourish the pure in thought.

Nonetheless, they can heal the wicked heart
That infected the pure in thought!

They bubble every second, minute,
And hour,
And set souls on fire.

Word, sound, and power
Can cause you to be hired
And get sufferers fired!

Word, sound, and power
Have caused freedom fighters to be expired!

MONOTONOUS CHILDREN

*Trapped in cycles of stagnation
With no way of exploring the power of thought.*

*Instead of creating metaphors, riddles, and parables,
They relish someone else's fables.*

*Instead of using their imagination,
They alternate and replicate from another man's
inspiration.*

*If writing, singing, or painting is not your gift,
Find your niche.*

*Oh, you shallow, sinful, plagiarizing thieves!
If you do not know how to find your niche,
Turn on the switch in yo' head
Seeking divine guidance;
He will open up your heavens.*

*Monotonous children!
Monotonous children!
Locked in cycles of stagnation, devouring originator
sayings.*

ENGLISH

The familiar voices asked me,
Were you a good English student in school?
I abruptly rebuffed, No!
I could not understand what the articulate
English teachers were teaching me.
I had no fondness for English,
Especially those who took me away on pirate
Ships.
To this very day, English is still my biggest
Perplexity.
You can ask Ms. Fibs, my English teacher,
And she will tell you that I,
The Irrepressible Drastic Carden Alphonso Michael,
Couldn't comprehend the technicality of the
grammatical bullshit!

Another Episode of Love

THE MAN WHO STRAYED

The man who strayed
Went the other way.
Good gracious God!
Why did he go that way,
Into the lower end, wobbling in stench?!

Sam's got to be mad
To reject Elaine's delicacy!

Good gracious God!
The honey in the V,
He tasted it not!
Sweet honey,
You are a therapy.

Thank heaven for sending you.
Thank heaven for your precious gifts
And tender hips,
Not to mention the delicious lips and tits.
He knows not what he's missed.
Thank heaven for your companionship.

PRETTY ROSE

There was a pretty rose in the garden.
The sexual predator never knew it was a thorn.
It blew from side to side, waving her head to
bystanders.
This fine, alluring beauty, fragrant, drowns nostrils.

Her intensity could not be avoided.
Sharky the predator got to have this irresistible
beauty,
Was overpowered by her gravity, fell as her prey.

He never knew the flesh could be disastrous.
Honey sweet in a mouth turns bitter in a belly.
Pretty Rose stole his heart, head, and money,
Then she ran and thought it was funny.

The charming beauty's words were enticing.
He never looked in her head before he put her in bed.
Money done, woman gone,
Only to leave Sharky with a broken heart!

WHEN SHE LEFT

I heard when she left,
He wept bitterly.
The little that he ate
He couldn't digest.
Man was restless,
Couldn't find the comfort of his bed.

Brokenhearted, needed mending.
Poor fellow's head was spinning.
Strong man started groaning,
Wobbled in sorrows.

The bully who used to terrify everybody
Sobbed bitterly!
Poor fellow rejected nourishment for his
Body.

Griever stumbled through the dark,
Looking for Millicent to comfort his heart.
Poor faller's bulky body turned sulky.
He drank buzz till the doctor had to save him from
Poison.
Dude was cocky and forward,
Brought to his knees by tiny Millie.

NEVER MINE

Never mine, you have been acting funny;
Still, you are my honey.

Never mine, you have been drifting lately;
Still, I will do anything that is possible
To have you next to me.

When you were not around,
I wore a frown.

When you were out of sight,
I said a prayer for my wife,
Hoping that I would hold her tight throughout
The night.

I PEN THIS NOTE

*I pen this note for a heart that
Lingers in my thoughts,
Waiting and hoping that our hearts might
Remerge.*

*That disappearance might reappear,
Hearts and mouths would mend, chatter, and
Giggle.*

*Hoping desertion would find solace,
Bleeding heart would stop aching.
Gloomy days might turn into sunshine rays.*

*Hoping Honey would forget about alimony,
Anticipating for her tender touch to cherish the
brokenhearted.*

*Magical arms, why won't you come and
Rub me with your palms?*

FOR MY ENDEARING QUEEN

*For you, my endearing queen.
A strong, vibrant and confident black woman,
Your pulsating rhythm ignites my fire.
You illuminate and stimulate me, even in my darkest
hours.
Your poise, erect as Nefertiti, tells me you are self
assured!*

*Beautiful black woman,
I shower abundance of praises for lifting me higher.*

AFTER A HARD DAY'S WORK

After a hard day's work,
I had another task with a fat
Bammy.
It was fluffy and juicy
And sweeter than candy.

Nothing could break my concentration
As I sizzled her sauce.

Nothing could break my heart
As I dove into her tart.
Nothing could break my thought
As I mesmerized her heart.

We squeezed tight, and I felt nice.
Sweetly she sings
As nuts and bolt grappled her thing.

Sweetly she sings
As nuts and bolt fling a ling.
Sweetly she sings
As nuts and bolt ding a ling.

COMFORT ME

*Comfort me in the bewilderment of
Desertion.
When I am lonely, sad, and blue and the
Elements are up against me,
Please never desert me.*

*When the nights are dark and dreary and
Curious eyes can't visualize Solomon's black and
comely son,
Rescue me.*

*When the mighty thunder bolts!
And the striking lightning flashes!
And terrestrial rain drops!
Oh kind and caring One,
Make it there without procrastinating.*

www.freedigitalphotos.net

The Journey of Love Continues

YOUR SENSATION

Your sensation is a sensual
Vibration!

It sends me up
On high.
You are my choice of drugs.

Popping pills, sniffing coke,
And drinking coke—
I have no taste for that.

Holding, cuddling, and spanking you—
That's what I love to do.

HONEYDEW

Hi, Honeydew.
Can I have a word with you?

You are enticing, tantalizing,
Alluring, and tempting;
Sassy, elegant, and classy.

It is a pity I cannot wrap my arms around your waist,
Whisper in your ear,
Mesmerize your thought,
And comfort your heart.

It is a pity I cannot dip my anchor into your crevice,
Plug your slit,
Push and give you all I got.

Honeydew,
It is a pity!

ANGEL OF THE NILE

Angel of the Nile,
Think I forget you?!
How can I forget a pretty thing like you?
How can I resent your charming beauty, the heart
men crave for?
Where can you hide when my eyes are tracking you?

Oh, you charming beauty,
Think you can escape these arms of mine?
Hell no!
The days these arms hold you, sweet endearing
beauty,
Not even the powers that control
Destiny would be able to undo these arms from
around you!

Angel of the Nile,
These arms are waiting for you!

CRICKET

Cricket, oh cricket, what a fine sport.

Even though I have not mastered the artistry
Of that game,
Nevertheless, girl, I would surely like to
Give you some good strokes!

Even though I might not be capable of
Hitting fours and sixes,
Still I would like to massage your hips,
Kiss your lips,
And lick your tits.

Even though I have not studied the rudiments of the
game,
Still, girl, I would like to discover your ingredient,
recipe, and secret taste.
Cricket, oh cricket, what a marvelous
Sport!

Searching for a Place to Call My Home

MY HOME

Is this place my home?
Where joy and happiness are bound with sorrow,
Where hopes and dreams are shattered for tomorrow,
Where envy and jealousy cluster in a sick, rotten
head!
Where hungry children get no supper, longing for a
piece of bread,
Where mothers and fathers squat in desolate places,
as stranded refugees!
Where nomads walk rugged terrain, to find a
temporary comfort zone,
Where tired, worn-out souls drop dead!
This place I roam, still searching for my home.

THE INVISIBLE ONE

*The invisible one passes by; I saw him on numerous
occasions.
We talked and rustled many a time.
He showed me a paradise beyond for edgy souls
And for those who were hounded for righteousness'
sake.
He said to me, "Be ye of good courage, for you were
found worthy to
Enter into glory.
When the time comes, I will humbly bow into your
Arms and say, 'Here I come you mysterious, invisible
one.'"*

A SOMBER MOOD

Mournful souls lift their voices.
They sighed and chattered for answers.
Wailers groped, yearning for the absent to fill their void.
Hearts ache, locked in a gaze, hoping that the Disappeared may relive the life she lived.

www.freefoto.com

SPRING

As spring arrived,
I took a breath of fresh air and gave a toast to
Nature's Lord.

I looked and saw arrays of colorful flowers,
Butterflies and honeybees synchronized.
Creeping ants, mosquitoes, and various species
Fascinated the eyes.

Birds frolicked, whistling,
Making melodies amongst the trees.

Then I said, Thank you, Lord, for the arrival of
spring.
Thank you for all creatures great and small.
Thank you for replenishing the earth.

www.digitalphoto.net

MEN OF STATUS

Men of status lost their virtue.
Strong, vibrant, pulsating men bound
Upon pirate ships in shackles
Sailed on seas like convicts.

Captured souls, they ravaged, whipped, and turned
Into ruins!

Muscular giants, mutilated and switched their
Sexual organs.
Sadly, the redefined African walks the plains of
Babylon
In high-heeled taps,
With lipstick and bulging tits.

WISE MAN

Wise man talks;
Fools bark.

Fools say to be wise,
You must blow your mouth like barking dogs
Making nonsensical noise.

When wise man keeps cool,
They say he is a fool.

When fools yap,
They say they're wise.

When wise man shuts his mouth, he is despised.
When fools growl, they are glorified.

Fools bark!
Wise man discusses the matter,
Defusing conflicts prudently.

Old Reflections

TRANQUIL NIGHT

*On a tranquil night,
I was home,*

Serenading to the soothing songs from a
Saxophone.
A little thereafter, I was obstructively disrupted from
The sentiment that came from the musical instrument.
Right away, I was taken by curiosity to see what
Was going on in my backyard.
I leaped and peeked through my window.
To my amazement, what I saw was fascinating to my
eyes.
It was Father Puss, pounding his striking hammer
rapturously on Mamma Puss's "cuscus."

While he fondled her,
She wailed!

As he blazed her tail,
She cried intensely!

As he set her soul on fire, causing a fiery contraction,
She cried in rage!

As she went insane,
He held her tight,
Whopping her backside!

Before he ejaculated,
I calculated the seconds—
1, 2, 3, 4, 5, sex!
He fires—bang!
She cried meow!!!!

When the fight was over,
He took off like a fugitive on the run.

I FLATUS

I flatus.
I flatus in the dark,
Sometimes in the bath
And when the dog barks.

I flatus in the light
And when I sleep at night.

You flatus,
Me flatus,
Everybody flatus!
Including the queen, pope,
And president.

Everybody poo-poo,
So why grumble when
I make my fart?
Oops! Excuse . . . me.
I flatus!

GLITTERY FACE

She glitters
A beaming face!
I was not in a mood to
Smirk
When I saw an inferno
Under her skirt.

She asked me,
"What's up, buddy?"
I said,
"Something looks funny, lady!"

She made a frown,
Twisted her head,
Then turned her frown into
Radiant light.

My intuition tells me
Be aware of her;
She is a gold digger
Who loots cash!

TWISTED AND TURNED

I twisted and turned upon my bed,
Hungry and thirsty for your love!
Life was a mess when you were not around.
I looked, and my pillow was an obstacle.
I called and said, "Hi."
You said, "Bye!"
I knocked upon your door,
And you said to go home.
Ah, my soul dips low!
I said,
"How could you be so mean in a time
Of need?"
Lonely and miserable was I.
Sleepless nights took hold of me.
Love was in the air.
You were not there.
While I quiver with boundless devotion,
You shiver with bitter emotion.
I said, "How could you be so cold?"
As I was left to freeze.
Then I fell into a doze and snored.
Nightmare took a hold of me.

I awoke from my snore and said,
"Nightmare, I want no more of you!
Sleepless nights, I've had enough of blues!
Life must go on.
To everything there is a season.
And everything happens for a reason.
Go away! I want no more of you."

SITTING DUCK

The sitting duck
Sat in the dark,
Waiting patiently to be plugged.
Her sense of virtue
She could not bear.
For two and a half years, she concealed her inner
beauty.
Eagles eyed her from afar;
Predators circled a vulnerable prey.
A garden of delicacies she exposed to voracious
mouths.
Predators feasted in a garden of saturated fat.
Fat, fluffy, tasty, and nourishing!
A bounty of love, she satisfied heart's desire.
The good man was absent; he got the news of shock
and disbelief.
In a wilderness of bewilderment, he exited to
confusion.
The hearts of men are delicate and weak as
malnourished babes.
The taste of honey is sweet to the mouth.
Oh, sometimes it can be funny.
To live the life of love is to cherish and not to perish.
The tales of love are told,
Bold,
And it is old.

GLAMOUR QUEEN

The glamour queen had no respect for the frigid cold,
She walked the streets of New York,
London,
Paris,
And Rome,
With her chest exposed to the brisk cold.

She was aware of pneumonia
Yet jeopardized her health
To frosty Arctic freeze!

Her fantasy was aimed at
Becoming a supermodel.

She flickered and dazzled along the walkway,
Wined and dined with the rich and shame-us.
Lived luxuriously
While drowning in misery.

She moved and grooved
With flair and glare,
Sold her soul for wretched gold.

Depriving herself of nutrients,
She became a case of anorexia.
Later she mourned and groaned when Doc told her
She was going to be a ghost!

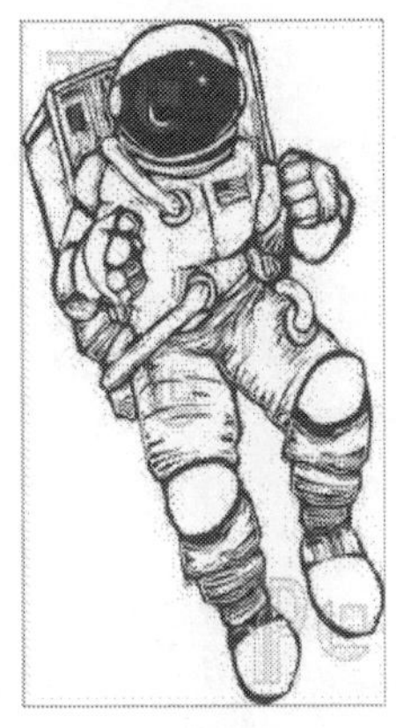

LOOK!

Hey, look! Look at the buffoon scientist!
He is on his way to the moon!

He is padded
In protective gear to tamper
With the elements in the atmosphere.

Look! He is zooming on his spaceship.
He soon lands on the moon
At twelve noon.

GHOSTS

*Ghosts dressed in white
In the dark of night
Make us fright.*

*They searched for blacks
In the late hours of the night.
They burned our houses and
Gouged our eyes
And hanged us up
Like monkeys in ah trees.*

They disregard old Granny and lynched Pappy.

*Ghosts dressed in white
In the late hours of the night
Had us terrified.*

ERR HE CRIES

Mamma!
Mamma!
Look ah zombie deh so!
'Ey want to catch me.

Mamma responded,
Child, stops your nonsense!

She then realized he was right.
Mamma consoled her child in her
Loving arms, wiping tears
From his eyes.

Demons I encountered couldn't destroy me!
I was once a victim of zombie atrocity.

THE SOUND OF R

Do you ever hear the sound of R? Well, I am going to tell you a story about that sound that has lingered in my brain for approximately three and a half decades.

When I was a little boy, it was a regular thing for me to check out the activities that were taking place in my close-knit community such as soccer, cricket, and the processions of Girl Guide and Boy Scout troops.

On one particular afternoon, as I roamed the street looking for something to intrigue the eyes, I came upon the scout troop parading through my neighborhood, doing their usual routines—hiking, drilling, and performing acrobatic moves.

These dudes wore attired as sharp as a cutting razor. They marched left–right, left–right like soldiers on parade. However, they were about to discipline one of their own for disorderly conduct. Apparently he had violated scout troop rules and was about to be whack for breaking the group's laws!

Those were the days when you could be reprimanded by a family member as well as a neighbor. There was a collective security that was valued by the folks who lived in my close-knit community.

Not even bullies could escape from a good whipping. Absolutely no one was an exception to the rules. You broke the rules, you would be whipped like a mule. That is exactly how my community was run.

In those days, morals and good behavior were the order of the day. Children respected their elders, and folks cared for each other. As a youngster, you dared not suck your teeth to an elder or else you might feel the wrath of a smacking hand landing on your mouth.

That afternoon, as I stood there watching and observing them parading, silence fell on their lips, stilling their voices. Fitzerland, the stern, unyielding scoutmaster, was serious like a bull. He yelled, "Stand at ease! Attention!" In a tense manner, the scouts halted and assumed a proper posture. Fitzerland flexed his rope from side to side.

He then began to expound as his troops listened attentively. After talking to his troops, he called out Alton, that unmannered, quick-tempered brat, and started to lecture him about his boorish behavior.

Moments after they started to whip the violator, when he got the first lash, he cringed and cried out, "R!!!!!!" The second lash he received throbbed upon his back like crackling thorns, and then everyone took turns beating the impolite faller. He wiggled and jiggled, cringed and twisted, wheeled and turned with his grimacing face, blustering with tears.

That day, I could have seen the rest of the troop take pleasure cording the disorderly offender. He gnashed his teeth and cried mercifully, "R!!!!!"

While this was going on, I, the curious observer, stood there patiently anticipating him to mutter, "S, H, I, T." But he murmured not even "N, O, P, Q, R, T, U." Yet all I could hear was "R!!!"

Oh yes, the striking rope continued to smack his back. He stood and cried emotionally. That afternoon, he surely got a well-deserved whipping for defying scout troop rules.

New Reflections

SEE THE PENDULUM

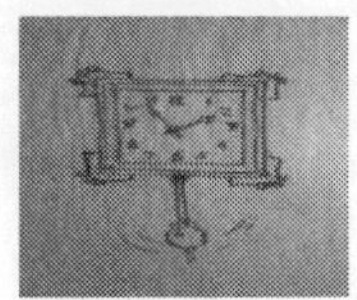

See the pendulum swinging?
Know that time is swiftly gliding.
Why are we fighting?
Why not give a brother a helping
Hand
Instead of putting him down?

Why do you piss me off?
Remember that time is short,
And we will soon part.

AS I AWOKE

As I awoke this morning,
I said a prayer for the pure in heart
To continue in righteous thoughts!
And to the acid heart,
I prayed for a change in deceitful thoughts.

www.gherp.com

DESPERATION HOWLS

Desperation howls from Death Valley
For the Mighty to deliver their souls from
Burning coals.

They sigh in pain and vent their frustrated voices
While the wicked turn their lofty faces.

They cram and jam into desolate places;
Only heaven knows their traces.

In that land of turmoil, pandemonium, and mayhem,
The ravished souls yearn and lament for stillness,
Yet they continue to stumble amongst perilous places.

They knows no heaven,
Cause their haunted souls faints in hell.

Desperation yowls from Death Valley
For the Mighty to deliver their souls from
Burning coals.

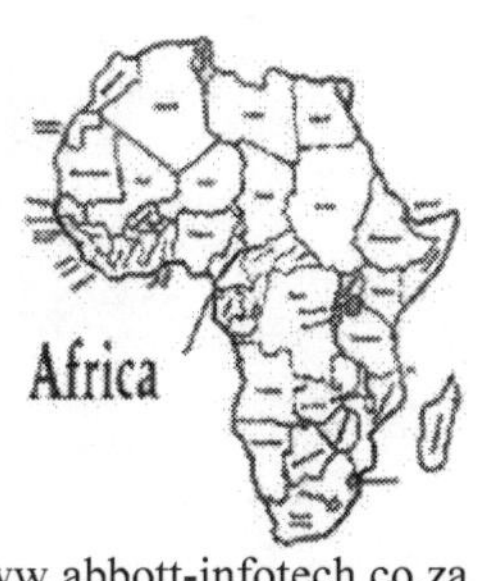

www.abbott-infotech.co.za

DOGS!

It sickens my heart to know that
Dogs are gods.
In some countries, they are more preferable
Than babies.
They live the high life while so many babies are
abandoned
And sometimes starve to death!

Dogs get pedicures and manicures,
Medical attention and pharmaceutical prescriptions,
Babysitters and daycare centers,
Bank accounts,
Treats and other amenities.
They assemble at recreational centers
And are pampered like young babies.

Dogs, oh dogs!
Thou art gods!!!!
In my book, dogs are dogs and should not be treated
equal to or above any human being.

www.digitalphoto.net

DANGEROUS MINDS

*Dangerous minds turn towns and cities
Into infernos.*

*Bombs dropping;
People incinerating.*

*Chaos and wars,
When would you depart?*

*Big military spenders,
When will the poor get the basic necessities
To satisfy their hearts' desires?*

*Liars and manipulators,
When will you sanctify your wretched souls?*

SOME AH THEM

Some say this, and some say that!
Some ah them blab, blab them bledy mouth!
Them love fo' chat!

Some ah them say them ah priest,
But them ah freaks!

Some ah them say them ah teach,
But them ah thieves!

Some ah them say them ah Muslim,
But them ah hoodlums!

Some ah them say them ah peacemakers,
But them ah warmongers.

Some ah them say them ah Christians,
Them bomb Afghanistan!

Some ah them ah say this, and some ah say that,
But all weh them ah do,
Them just love fo' chat!

EYES ARE WATCHING

Eyes are watching, mouths are talking.
Keep talking,
Keep talking.

While their mouths chat crap, and bangs me furiously.
I tell furious mouths, "Don't hit me so hard,
Please have some mercy."

Keep talking,
Keep talking.
I heard you barking,
Woof! Woof! Woof! Woof!!!!!

THAT FALLER

That faller named egotist, worse than a bitch!
He wants to be cricketer, footballer, and runner!
Dub poet, writer, and philosopher!
Singer, painter, and sculptor!

In the rat race,
He becomes critic, inspector, and dissector!
Oppressor, backbiter, and victimizer!
Cultural ambassador and damager!

The conniving egotist,
racketeer, swindler, and fiddle!
Covetous, envious,
and bad minded!
Hateful, lustfully grudging!
With such ah bad rap, he is a rat!

With such a lengthy portfolio, I tell the egotist, "I've had
it with you!
Kiss my rear and get out here!"

THIS ONE!

This one is for Linton Crazy Johnson,
De dub poet inna London!

Linton, me want you to hear this, man!
Yo come inside a Rasta camp.
Rasta gee yo what them gat.
Them nourish you with the sweet militant reggae vibe!
Them teach yo how fi chant poetry to rub-a-dub.
When yo done suck Rasta blood, yo turn around and bite
Rasta like viper!
Ah preach yo Marxist ideology,
'Bout yo na dig Selassie!
Telling me that Rasta romanticizes Selassie!
But when ah check it out, you sanctimoniously worship
them white guys,
Marx, Lenin, and Stalin!

Linton, yo rally let me down, brother!
Kwesi, the things you said about Rasta mek me wonder if
yo crazy!
Yo even denounce Holy Mount Zion,
Yet yo glorify de mosquitoes inna Moscow!
But ah hope when yo well run dry and yo deceased
friends Marx and Lenin can't quench yo thirst,
Na batter come ah Rasta yard and hound like hungry
dog!
Go ah Russia and look fo Markie ghost!

LINTON CRAZY JOHNSON!

One more thing me want yo fi know brother,
Yo think say dat bloody Russian white dude different than
De capitalistic American white guy?
If yo think so, yo just naïve, man!
Yo forget in 1934 when Stalin turn him backs on the
Blacks inna South Africa?

Marxist enthusiastic!
Me never hear yo mention Garvey, Martin Luther King,
or Nanie's name,
'Cause yo get caught up inna Cold War affair
'Bout dem demons dat almost set de world on fire!

Brother B, me na hear yo say nothing when de hungry
Russians them, who craved for freedom and liberty, tore
down Felix Dzerzhinsky iconic statue?
Me never hear yo say nothing when the KGB and CIA
agents turnout to be best of friends!
What yo goin to do, when the Kremlin, crumble down?

Linton, Linton, my brother, I write this one just for you.
Long live the black liberation struggle!
Long live the rejected and the despised Rastas!
Long live the children of Selassie I!
Long live Jah Rastafar I!

THE LEADERS
OF THE WORLD

The leaders of the world talk about peace!
When is there going to be peace in the Middle East?
When is there going to peace between dissident
And president,
Outlaws, conformists, reformers, and
nonconformists?
Peacemakers, freedom fighters, and assassins?

Nevertheless,
Love is what it takes to cease wars and turmoil in our
Troubled world.
Love is what it would take to unify this fragmented
world,
The mediator between agitators and oppressors!

One love!
To all political gangsters,
Thugs,
Rivals,
Tyrants, and heads of governments.

One love to all rebels who fight to enjoy a piece of the
pie
Right here on Earth!

GOVERNMENTS SUCK!

*They purchase Cadillacs
With the poor man's bucks.*

*They build rockets
And run rackets.*

*Their words are smooth,
Yet their action crude!*

*Beneath their smile looms deceit,
Dishonesty, and trickery.*

*They click and clique
In secret places
And pledge allegiance to fulfill the mission of
Lucifer.*

*They lie with a passion
And never think about repentance!*

*Governments are great technicians!
Governments are the great dividers!
Governments are bandits!*

MY JEWEL

My tropical jewel is at a crossroads.
Caught up in a web of political disorder,
Where do I stand?
Neutral between the intricacies of opposition
Party and ruling party,
Between either and neither,
Between the ruling class and upper frauds,
Between deceivers and manipulators,
Plutocrats and aristocrats.

In the heat of the battle,
I stand in the midst of thieves.
However, I stand with Jah Almighty.
He never leaves, tricks, or deceives me.

My jewel, St, Vincent and the Grenadines,
Are at a crossroads, caught in a web of
Political Conflicts!

NO MORE TRIBALISM INNA SVG

Tranquil island me used to know,
Wha happen to yo?
Why so much a blood run inside ah yo?
All at sudden, yo natives start to loot and shoot!
Yo have bad man upper Largo, bad man inna ghetto,
and bab man down ah Chateau!
Quite frequently me see undertakers rush with them,
gone ah cemetery!

A nation at war needs to be calm!
Youths from Chateau, Bagga, Kingstown, and
Georgetown,
Come, lay we reason together!
Come, let we have a talk about black liberation,
Defusing the tension of the white man indoctrination!
Listen to the voices of Garvey, Nkrumah, and Kenyatta,
Echoing the sentiment of unity and
Harmony unambiguously!

Now, this poem is not about wining and grinding on
Patsy bumper (Butt)!
But this poem is about the deterioration of Yuloo!
The moral decadence cand bad vibes we hear every day!
The deterioration needs serious attention urgently to
awaken the slumbering masses' mentality,
Particularly the youth who lack direction!

Yea, I beckon the political gurus
of Green, Yellow, and Red party;
Tone down yo political rhetoric!
We don't need more tribalism inna SVG!

I caution Anessia and Jomo;
Forming two other political party inna SVG
Would deepen the polarization in this divided nation!
I plea with the youths fo put the guns down and flee
gangsterism!
Every day you run up and down inna Hirrona like
buccaneers, ah loot an ah shoot!
Yo na have no respect for God, much less fo dog!
Every time yo head get hot, you mutilate and assassinate!
Yo so heartless, yo even rape and murder Granny!
Oh Jah, what a go on inna St, Vincent?

Lawless gangbanging youths,
me want you fo know, gangsterism derived from
Buccaneer's conception!
Too much blood done shed already on them plantation;
it is time to cease from black-on-black violence inna disya
land!

Black and comely people,
The spirits of Chatoya, Macintosh, and Joshua is talking
to you,
Reminding you of the price they paid!

Dis Jacky inna SVG, play this one for the nation!
It's a curse for men to trivialize paltriness!
Ignorant blind the psyche!
Corruption creates anarchy;
Perversions desecrate a blessed nation!
Ruthlessness causes an imbalance!

St, Vincent, where do you stand in this dispensation?
Living, breading the air of contamination!
Oh Jah, send a lightning rod to smite this duppy
vibration!

Rise up, St, Vincent; shake off the tainted blight.
Colonialism we must despise.
Let no barriers rip us apart!
We need oneness inna St, Vincent!
We don't need more political tribalism inna St, Vincent!

A BRIGHTER VISION FOR TOMORROW

What would it feel like to live in a world free from wars,
Insecurity, and impurities? Where there wouldn't
Be any hackers and attackers,
Bankers and swindlers,
Sorrows and troubles,
Demagogues and despots,
Traitors and conspirators,
Brokers and Wall Street hustlers,
Stress and anguish,
Malice and hatred,
Greed and gluttony,
Mobsters and thugs,
Buccaneers and savagery,
Pirates and looters,
Hijackers and kidnappers,
Hoodlums and gangbangers,
Bandits and convicts,
Heathens and she-dens,
False prophets and Pharisees,
Tyrants and dictators,
Guns and bombs,

Clansmen and tribalists,
Genocide and holocausts,
Haters and warmongers,
Barbarians and castrators,
Fakers and con artists,
Envy and jealousy,
Snakes and backbiters,
Wolves and leopards,
Oppressors and slave drivers,
Demons and zombies,
Vampires and bloodsuckers,
Devils and sinners,
Ghosts and spooks,
Rich and poor,
Disadvantaged and underprivileged,
Orphans and pariahs?

What it will be like to live in a world with peace and
harmony,
Without pedophiles and psychopaths,
Coke sniffers and pork eaters,
Heroin and methamphetamine,
Hoaxers and impostors,
Poverty-stricken and malnourished,
Hypocrites and parasites,
Tribulation and humiliation,
Courthouse and jailhouse,
Civil rights activists and arbitrators,
Injustice and exploitation,
Insurrections and perpetrators,
Instigators and troublemakers,
Desperation and segregation,
Racism and bigotry,
Rednecks and prejudice,

Nazism and white supremacy,
Egotists and swell-headed,
Cocky and arrogant,
Political upheaval and religious warfare?
When will these things come to an end?